P9-DCP-416

16 95

Trademarks of the '60s & '70s

Trademarks of the '60s & '70s

by Tyler Blik

introduction by Philip B. Meggs

CHRONICLE BOOKS

SAN FRANCISCO

Copyright ©1998 by Tyler Blik. All rights reserved.
No part of this book may be reproduced in any form
without written permission from the publisher.

Printed in Hong Kong.

Library of Congress Cataloging-in-
Publication Data:

Blik, Tyler.
        Trademarks of the '60s and '70s/by Tyler Blik;
introduction by Philip B. Meggs.
        p.   cm.
        ISBN 0-8118-1698-2 (pbk.)
        1. Commercial art—United States—Themes,
        motives. 2. Trademarks—United States—
        History—20th Century—Themes, motives.
        I. Title.
NC998.5.A1B57   1998
745.2'0973'09046—dc21   97-9340
                                             CIP

Distributed in Canada by Raincoast Books
8680 Cambie Street
Vancouver, B.C. V6P 6M9

10 9 8 7 6 5 4 3 2 1

Chronicle Books
85 Second Street
San Francisco, California
94105

Web Site: www.chronbooks.com

To my wife Sonya Devine and
our son Aleksander.

Acknowledgements

I would like to thank all of the graphic designers of this era, who provide us with a glimpse of America's popular cultural past. I would especially like to thank my dear friend Eric Baker for all of our experiences we have shared together. I am indebted to design historian Philip Meggs, Bill LeBlond and Julia Flagg at Chronicle Books and my friends and colleagues that have contributed to the process of putting this project together. To Gary Benzel for his steady contributions and design support. Many thanks to Carlos Gutierrez, Todd St. John, Erin Hall, Ken Soto, Ron Fleming, Carolyn Springer, Kim Dropik, and the staff of the San Diego Public Library.

Tyler Blik

Table of Contents

Introduction

Trademarks are the linchpins of contemporary communication. These small graphic designs can signify a particular cola drink, television network, or manufacturer. They differentiate each company, product, or service from its competitors. Trademarks become miniature worlds that store memories, passions, and reputations in the minds of employees, customers, and stockholders. From corner restaurants to multinational corporations whose activities circumnavigate a shrinking planet, every organization has to have one. These crown jewels of business are the most public and recognizable faces of far-flung conglomerates.

Each decade a new army of trademarks marches forth to join the thousands already in use. Many new trademarks survive the mercurial fashions of their day and become part of our stable of familiar icons. At the same time, hundreds of trademarks are forced into early retirement as companies go out of business, replace an obsolete trademark with a more contemporary design, or vanish in a leveraged buyout or merger. Others are terminated when their companies pass into chapter eleven, while still others retire because their companies outgrow them by expanding into new markets. A company might even change its name and trademark after widespread negative publicity because the old mark has become a lightning rod attracting public scorn.

The 1960s and 1970s were vintage decades for trademark design. Corporations learned about the importance of visual identity as a new breed of graphic designer taught them that identity was something they could design and control. Modernism was on the march, and it seemed an appropriate style to express the advanced technology of multinational corporations. At the same time, grassroots entrepreneurs designed their own logos, or commissioned local art students to whip out vernacular designs. Pop art and psychedelia expanded the range of acceptable design motifs.

Each trademark should be a new and unique design, that separates itself from the others, but all too often trademark design becomes the art of the cliché. Familiar motifs–globes, suns, flowing hair, big-headed little cartoon folks, and abstracted initials–are recycled again and again. When designers struggle to give each mark an original visual presence, however they bring forth logos that are eccentric, beautiful, or unexpected.

Many of the designers presented here have survived to become important elements of our graphic lexicon. Although others did not survive their time, they still proclaim the tastes, design styles, and social preoccupations of their day. We are indeed fortunate that Tyler Blik has undertaken the exhaustive archeological research necessary to bring this anthology together. Collectively these trademarks express the spirit of a very recent but now bygone time.

A twinge of nostalgia will be raised for those who lived through the social unrest of the turbulent sixties and the "stagflation" of the seventies. A younger generation will find an expression of the indefinable spirit of a time and place they never knew, now collected and made permanent in this handsome volume. Decades from now, someone will pull this book from a library shelf and experience a surge of excitement over these wonderful graphic marks. Perhaps that person will even borrow a form, motif, or idea to replenish logo design in some future time and place. But then, we've always known one thing books do very well, they establish a dialogue between generations.

Philip B. Meggs

Corporate America

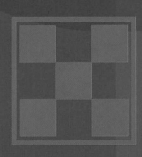

By the 1960s, the postwar production that began in the late 1940s was at full speed. American companies and organizations were expanding their manufacturing and services on a global scale. Conveying a company's image across many different cultural boundaries now became the job not only of designers, but of marketing consultants, focus groups, and quite possibly, a board of directors. The trademarks produced from these decades are a geometric distillation of the multiple personalities and disciplines of each corporation.

Early trademarks from '60s embraced a simplification of letter forms, typically within a field with a bold geometric shape or form. In Paul Rand's succinct extraction of the Westinghouse logo, for example, the viewer reads the initial and, at the same time, the type of business the company provides.

The synthesis of the corporate image became even more apparent in the '70s. Graphic designers continued to break down line and shapes to their bare minimum. The modest checkerboard of Ralston Purina (page 25) suggests nothing of the pet food business it is in. It refers rather, to its country, agricultural, and live-stock roots. Many of these symbols bear bold solid shapes that are often repeated and mirrored, subliminally implying the strength and stability behind corporate America's interests.

1960
MOTOROLA, INC.

Chicago, Illinois
Radio and television receiving and transmitting
apparatus

1971
EASTMAN KODAK COMPANY

Rochester, New York
Film and film-related products

1961
COLUMBIA BROADCASTING SYSTEM, INC.

New York, New York
Phonograph records

1967
WESTINGHOUSE ELECTRIC CORPORATION

Pittsburgh, Pennsylvania
Electrical apparatus, machines, and supplies

1963
DOUGLAS AIRCRAFT COMPANY, INC.

Santa Monica, California
Aircraft

1960
**AMERICAN HOME AND LIGHTING
INSTITUTE**

Chicago, Illinois
Residential lighting fixtures

1975
**SOCIETY OF TEACHERS OF FAMILY
MEDICINE**

Kansas City, Missouri
Association services

1962
**ASSOCIATION OF BETTER BUSINESS
BUREAUS, INC.**

New York, New York
Investigative and information services relative to
business

1971
PARASOL PRESS, LTD.

New York, New York
Books and portfolios of original lithographs

1967
STOP AND SHOP, INC.

Boston, Massachusetts
Supermarket services

1963
DELCON CORPORATION

Palo Alto, California
Electrical measuring devices

1967
COLOR MONITOR CORPORATION

Rye, New York
Reproducing documents and papers

1965
LIBERTY CARTON COMPANY

Minneapolis, Minnesota
Insulated shipping cartons

1968
DIAMOND NATIONAL CORPORATION

New York, New York
Wooden spoons, forks, and stirrers

1962
GENERAL FOODS CORPORATION

White Plains, New York
Processed foods

1962
SAFECO INSURANCE COMPANY OF AMERICA

Seattle, Washington
Underwriting of insurance

1963
CASTLE, LTD.

Los Angeles, California
Envelopes, writing paper, and correspondence
cards

1967
WESCOR CORPORATION

Hawesville, Kentucky
Semichemical corrugating medium material

1960
LAWRY'S FOODS, INC.

Los Angeles, California
Powdered dip mixes, seasonings, and salad
dressings

1966
THE ISALY DAIRY CORPORATION

Youngstown, Ohio
Retail food store services

1974
**HUNTINGTON MECHANICAL
LABORATORIES, INC.**

Mountain View, California
Construction services

1971
NALEWS, INC.

Gilford, New Hampshire
Construction services

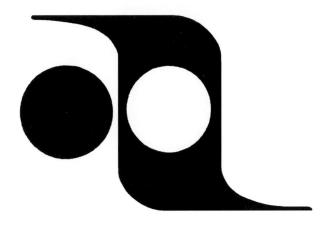

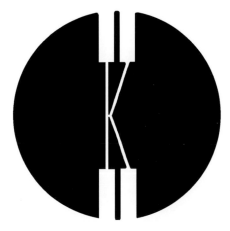

1965
AMES AMERICAN

North Easton, Massachusetts
Cleaning and surfacing of rolls used on
papermaking and textile machinery

1969
ART METAL-KNOLL CORPORATION

New York, New York
Architectural and engineering planning and design

1968
NATIONAL NUCLEAR CORPORATION

Palo Alto, California
Nuclear reactor consulting services

1972
THE QUAKER OATS COMPANY

Chicago, Illinois
Ready-to-eat cereals

1968
OPEN ROAD INTERNATIONAL, INC.

St. Louis, Missouri
Arranging travel tours

1966
NATIONAL WORK CLOTHES RENTAL

Elizabeth, New Jersey
Rental services

1967
BURLINGTON INDUSTRIES, INC.

New York, New York
Finished fabrics used in men's, women's, and
children's apparel

1974
**THE AMERICAN FREEDOM TRAIN
FOUNDATION, INC.**

Dedham, Massachusetts
Programs, and activities for the commemoration
of the United States Bicentennial

Growise

Sunkist

1978
GRO GROUP, INC.
Waltham, Massachusetts
Advertising and promotional services

1965
HUNT FOODS, INC.
Fullerton, California
Tomato products

1969
JOINT CLING PEACH ADVISORY BOARD
San Francisco, California
Canned California cling peaches

1976
SUNKIST GROWERS, INC.
Sherman Oaks, California
Fruit and fruit juices

1967
CONTAINER CORPORATION OF AMERICA
Chicago, Illinois
Paperboard boxes

1964
THE AMERICAN TOBACCO COMPANY
New York, New York
Cigarettes

1975
DANN IL MORRIS
Portland, Oregon
Backpacks

1972
NUTRITION LABORATORIES, INC.
Portland, Oregon
Feed supplement including bacteria culture

1964
MARINE MIDLAND CORPORATION
Buffalo, New York
General banking services

1976
**AMERICAN REVOLUTION
BICENTENNIAL ADMINISTRATION**
Washington, D.C.
Commemoration of American Bicentennial

1977
LABEL ART, INC.
Wilton, New Hampshire
Labels

1965
MERCK & CO., INC.
Rahway, New Jersey
Pharmaceutical preparations

1974
PHILADELPHIA '76, INC.

Philadelphia, Pennsylvania
Developing and directing plans, programs,
and activities for the commemoration of the
Bicentennial

1976
GOOLAGONG

Cleveland, Ohio
Clothes

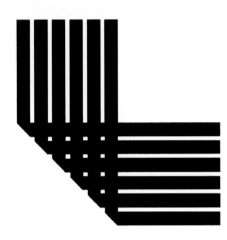

1971
LARSON ENTERPRISES, INC.

Los Angeles, California
Photographic light-reflecting devices

1964
THE WOOL BUREAU, INC.

New York, New York
Products made wholly or predominantly of wool

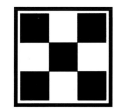

1969
**THE TORRINGTON MANUFACTURING
COMPANY**

Torrington, Connecticut
Devices for propelling air and other gases

1970
THE RUSTIX

Rochester, New York
Entertainment services

1967
**METROPOLITAN LIFE INSURANCE
COMPANY**

New York, New York
Insurance and annuity underwriting

1978
RALSTON PURINA COMPANY

St. Louis, Missouri
Pet and animal products

1974
MC CARRAN INTERNATIONAL AIRPORT

Las Vegas, Nevada
Airport and travel services

1966
SEA AND SKI CORPORATION

Millbrae, California
Sunglasses

1970
UNITED STATES AUTOMOBILE ASSOCIATION

San Antonio, Texas
Insurance underwriting and estate planning

1970
BANK OF AMERICA NATIONAL TRUST & SAVINGS ASSOCIATION

San Francisco, Califorina
Commercial bank sevices

1979
TRANSAMERICA CORPORATION

San Francisco, California
Insurance and investment services

1974
TELEDYNE, INC.

Los Angeles, California
Aircraft navigation instruments

1969
CROWN ZELLERBACH CORPORATION

San Francisco, California
Paper products

1977
CONTROL DATA CORPORATION

Minneapolis, Minnesota
Paper goods and printed matter

1961
WEYERHAEUSER COMPANY

Tacoma, Washington
Boxes

1977
BERGSTROM PAPER COMPANY

Neenah, Wyoming
Paper made from recycled papers

1967
SECURITY FIRST NATIONAL BANK

Los Angeles, California
Bank services

1972
CONTINENTAL AIRLINES, INC.

Los Angeles, California
Air transportation

1970
NORTH AMERICAN ROCKWELL CORPORATION

Pittsburgh, Pennsylvania
Structural parts and components for aerospace
and weapon defense

1969
ALLIED VAN LINES, INC.

Broadview, Illinois
Packing, storage, and transportation of goods

1975
MOUNTAIN BELL
Denver, Colorado
Long distance customer service

1977
VITA PLUS, INC.
Las Vegas, Nevada
Dietary supplements

1970
JAPAN WORLD EXPOSITION
Osaka, Japan
1970 World Exposition

1976
CHESTEL, INC.
Chester, Connecticut
Telephone communication systems

1968
AMERICAN BROADCASTING COMPANIES, INC.
New York, New York
Radio broadcasting

1966
ELGAR ELECTRONICS CORPORATION
San Diego, California
AC line conditioners

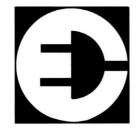

1977
FIRST TENNESSEE NATIONAL CORPORATION

Memphis, Tennessee
Banking services

1975
BAY AREA ASSOCIATION FOR SUICIDE PREVENTION

San Francisco, California
Suicide prevention

1974
MICHAEL BUSINESS MACHINES CORPORATION

New York, New York
Desktop collators for sorting and distributing papers

1960
ALLSTATE INSURANCE COMPANY

Skokie, Illinois
Underwriting of insurance risks

1969
ANALOG TECHNOLOGY CORPORATION

Pasadena, California
Pulse height analyzers and gas chromatographs

1975
NATIONAL CONGRESS OF PARENTS AND TEACHERS

Chicago, Illinois
Association services

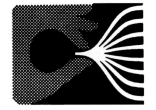

1979
**AMERICAN TELEPHONE AND
TELEGRAPH COMPANY**
New York, New York
Telephone directories

1974
UNITED WAY OF AMERICA
Alexandria, Virginia
Charitible foundation

The sixties brought an air of energetic idealism to an America that was no longer content with social norms. Typographic slogans shouted as they questioned authority, while their styles varied from the naive to the elegant. Product names sometimes carried whimsical phrases; others spoke of a life far from what "reality" had to offer. Some of the typographic solutions expressed the notion that one's life could be changed through the identity of the trademark.

With more and more competition in the marketplace, a trademark's customized typographic letterforms became evermore critical in delivering a company's unique positioning of its product or service. Businesses recognized the importance of aligning themselves with the most current cultural vernacular, and products like Perk-Up, Right On and Our Thing became reflections of an American attitude.

Many typographical trademarks of the late sixties and early seventies imitated the popular rock-concert posters of the time. Typography took on amorphous distortions, imitating the work of artists like Stanley Mouse, Rick Griffin, and Alton Kelly. These logotypes sometimes conformed to familiar shapes, resembling hearts, lips, and feet. Was this a clue to consult our inner psyche? More and more, designers were refining typographic treatments so that their appeal hit the mark of the consumer's fancy, indirectly reflecting the company's image and style.

Typography

1976
NATIONAL PRESTO INDUSTRIES, INC.

Eau Claire, Wisconsin
Domestic electric cooking devices

1972
FIVE-Y MANUFACTURING COMPANY

Inman, Kansas
Riding power lawn mowers

1964
HAWK MODEL COMPANY, INC.

New York, New York
Plastic juvenile luggage and school bags

1976
CLAEYS CANDY, INC.

South Bend, Indiana
Boxed chocolate candy

1969
SOUTHWESTERN APPAREL, INC.

Garland, Texas
Women's slacks, blouses, skirts, dresses, and
jackets

1962
THE PEPPERMINT COMPANY

Philadelphia, Pennsylvania
Hoop made of flexible or resilient material and
used for dancing the Twist

1968
OLYMPIC CORN PRODUCTS, INC.

Spokane, Washington
Batter-encased frankfurters on sticks

1962
**THE HUBBARD-HALL CHEMICAL
COMPANY**

Waterbury, Connecticut
Fertilizers

1961
CROWN ZELLERBACH CORPORATION
San Francisco, California
Polyethylene-coated paper bags

1965
GARWOOD L. DONNELSON
Greenwood Station, Nebraska
Rug cleaner

1966
MIDLAND SHOE COMPANY
St. Louis, Missouri
Women's shoes

1967
LORD JIM, INC.
Madison, Wisconsin
Men's clothing

1972
SECOND LOOK, INC.
King of Prussia, Pennsylvania
Retail women's clothing store services

1964
TYER RUBBER CORPORATION
Andover, Massachusetts
Stocking-foot waders, shirts, pants, parkas,
jackets, and raincoats

Lord Jim

1969
ARROW PLYWOOD CORPORATION
Belmont, Massachusetts
Plywood and construction materials

1965
FIVE NOTES, INC.
Milwaukee, Wisconsin
Entertainment services

1964
TOWER OF PIZZA
Ramsey, New Jersey
Calzone

1972
COSBY HODGES MILLING COMPANY
Birmingham, Alabama
Horse feed

1960
CHARLES A. CRETE
Marysville, California
Multivitamin preparation for children

1963
COLLEGE-TOWN OF BOSTON
Boston, Massachusetts
Women's junior size sportswear

1962
MARCHAL, INC.
New York, New York
Precious and costume jewelry

1965
ACME MARKETS, INC.
Philadelphia, Pennsylvania
Hair spray and shampoo

1961
SUSAN THOMAS
New York, New York
Rayon fabrics made into finished clothing

1969
NU-LIVING, INC.
North Royalton, Ohio
Cosmetic face and body freshening

1977
MATHER FEDERAL CREDIT UNION
Sacramento, California
Banking services

1973
PLAYGIRL FIGURE SALONS
South Bend, Indiana
Conducting women's exercise workshops

miss DiOrsini

Beautiful Moods

Fabergé Organics

SonaRi

1978
WALGREEN LABORATORIES, INC.

Deerfield, Illinois
Deodorant

1967
NATIONAL SHOES, INC.

New York, New York
Children's and misses' shoes

1972
WILLIAMHOUSE-REGENCY, INC.

New York, New York
Greeting cards

1977
FABERGÉ, INC.

New York, New York
Cosmetics and toilet preparations

1965
AIMS FOUNDATIONS, INC.

New York, New York
Women's undergarments

1970
THE SAMGAMON COMPANY

Taylorville, Illinois
Greeting cards

1976
**NATIONAL AERONAUTICS AND
SPACE ADMINISTRATION**

Washington, D.C.
U.S. Government space exploration program

1976
PEPSICO, INC.

Purchase, New York
Soft drinks and syrups

1976
AMERICAN CAN COMPANY

Greenwich, Connecticut
Disposable eating utensils

1977
THE GAP STORES, INC.

San Francisco, California
Retail clothing store service

1976
NICHIBEL FUJI CYCLE CO., LTD.

Tokyo, Japan
Bicycle and structural parts

1970
HANES CORPORATION

Winston-Salem, North Carolina
Women's hosiery and pantyhose

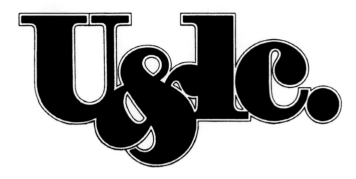

1975
**INTERNATIONAL TYPEFACE
CORPORATION**
New York, New York
Periodical journal

1967
AVANT-GARDE MEDIA, INC.
New York, New York
Magazine

1976
BEANS, INC.

Santa Ana, California
Restaurant services

1976
CITICORP

New York, New York
Leasing space for commercial outlets

1971
BIT, INC.

Natick, Massachusetts
Installation and repair services for computers

1968
BRATTLE FILMS, INC.

Cambridge, Massachusetts
Men's and women's wearing apparel

1971
RJR FOODS, INC.

New York, New York
Canned prepared desserts

1976
BERGSTROM PAPER COMPANY

Neenah, Wisconsin
Offset, bond, printing, and writing papers made
from recycled paper

1973
BROCO PRODUCTS, INC.

Cleveland, Ohio
General purpose liquid detergents

1973
**THE GENERAL BOARD OF EVANGELISM
OF THE UNITED METHODIST CHURCH**

Nashville, Tennessee
Religious quarterly publication

1975
THE LOVE COMPANY

Sioux Falls, South Dakota
All-purpose cleaning preparations

1977
FABERGÉ, INC.

New York, New York
T-shirts

1974
THE WHIZ KIDS

Chicago, Illinois
Artistic design of commercial printing media

1977
HUB DISTRIBUTING, INC.

Ontario, California
Clothing

1971
ACTIVE PRODUCTS, INC.

San Francisco, California
Construction toy

1973
INVER HOUSE DISTILLERS, LTD.

Philadelphia, Pennsylvania
Whiskey

1972
WILLIAMHOUSE-REGENCY, INC.

New York, New York
Greeting cards

1973
SPICE, INC.

Topeka, Kansas
Magazine

1973
THE POP INNS

Chico, California
Soft drinks

1966
ARTHUR TAYLOR LEE

Los Angeles, California
Musical entertainment services

1971
DOVE
Syracuse, New York
Entertainment services

1972
THE PILLSBURY COMPANY
Minneapolis, Minnesota
Drinking straws

1968
C & F PRODUCTS OF SAN FRANCISCO, INC.
San Francisco, California
Toy or amusement-type spectacles with kaleidoscopic lens

1969
FREEMEN ENTERPRISES, INC.
New York, New York
Men's clothing

1975
LANSCO ASSOCIATED MILLS, LTD.
Southbury, Connecticut
Socks

1967
CITRUS CENTRAL, INC.
Orlando, Florida
Frozen concentrated orange juice

1969
PRECISION MERCHANDISE, INC.

Brooklyn, New York
Cologne

1970
WEMBLY INDUSTRIES, INC.

New Orleans, Louisiana
Men's neckwear

1974
THE JACOBS CORPORATION

Boulder, Colorado
Leather goods

1967
FIRST GIRL, INC.

Chicago, Illinois
Supplying temporary help

1972
FIELD HOTEL CORPORATION

Clearwater Beach, Florida
Cocktail lounge and beverage services

1968
PELLON CORPORATION

New York, New York
Textile fabrics

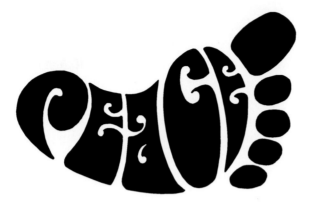

1969
M.T.S. PRODUCTIONS
Cincinnati, Ohio
Automobile bumper stickers

1969
**EDUCATIONAL RESEARCH
ASSOCIATES, INC.**
Palo Alto, California
Consultation and advice in internal administrative
systems of schools

Animals

In graphic renderings, man has always paid homage to the animal kingdom, both domestic and wild. Characteristics of animal behavior often provided a backdrop to a company's personality as animals became spokespersons (or spokes-animals) creating an ongoing dialogue between the company and consumer. A hip Charlie the Tuna, dressed in sunglasses and beret, told the public that it was cool to eat canned tuna fish; and animated cartoon characters such as Walter Lantz's Woody Woodpecker sold products like chewing gum. These animal characters, with their human-like qualities, touched consumers' humor and emotions.

Other more stylized characters of the 1960s and 1970s became symbols by expressing qualities of a company inherent within a particular animal. The Merrill Lynch bull, for example, stands ready to charge and displays the corporation's strength and tenacity and its reputation for providing sound financial investments. The elegant, swirling line work of the Easterling Company's butterfly emulates the qualities found in their refined and graceful china tableware. Whether it is the intelligence of an owl, the toughness of a rhino, or the beauty of a peacock that is incorporated, the inclusion of animal attributes in trademarks draws on powerful intuitions within human psyches.

1966
ABERDEEN MANUFACTURING CORPORATION

New York, New York
Umbrellas and parts thereof

1968
YOUNG WORLD CORPORATION

Washington, D.C.
Computer dating service

CLUB BASTILLE

Jolly Tiger

plaf

Kangaroo

1966
GEIGY CHEMICAL CORPORATION
Ardaley, New York
Sponges

1978
SAMBO'S RESTAURANTS, INC.
Santa Barbara, California
Restaurant services

1969
CARDINAL VENDING COMPANY
Cleveland, Ohio
Vending machines

1969
TRIMFOOT COMPANY
St. Louis, Missouri
Infants' shoes

1973
WILLIAM C. HUNT
Issaquah, Washington
Multipurpose cooking assembly

1967
EDDIE BAUER
Seattle, Washington
Waterfowl decoys

1960
HAYES SPRAY GUN COMPANY

Pasadena, California
Service kit comprising replacement and repair
parts for garden spray guns

1960
BIRMINGHAM TIN SHOP

Birmingham, Alabama
Small gasoline powered autos

1972
ANN E. WELCH DOG TRAINING SCHOOL

Cincinnati, Ohio
Canine obedience training

1976
SAMBO'S RESTAURANTS, INC.

Santa Barbara, California
Restaurant services

1960
LAMAR S.R.L.

Buenos Aires, Argentina
Canned food for dogs

1977
MCMULLEN GROVE COMPANY

Riverview, Florida
Tropical fish and aquatic plants

Dignifried Chicken

1960
ALLIGATOR COMPANY

St. Louis, Missouri
Raincoats

1976
HOST INTERNATIONAL, INC.

Santa Monica, California
Raw chicken and chicken parts

1965
THE RED BARN SYSTEM

Fort Lauderdale, Florida
Chicken dinners

1968
CHICK-FIL-A, INC.

Hapeville, Georgia
Frozen chicken parts

1965
CALIFORNIA WESTERN RAILROAD

Fort Bragg, California
Steam-powered rail transportation of persons and
property

1975
FRITO-LAY, INC.

Dallas, Texas
Cheese-flavored corn chips

1977
FARMSTEAD INDUSTRIES
Waterloo, Iowa
Prefabricated livestock pens

1971
GRO-KOTEL, INC.
Santa Rosa, California
Dog food

1962
STAR-KIST FOODS, INC.
Terminal Island, California
Canned fish

1965
THE COCA-COLA COMPANY
Atlanta, Georgia
Canned fruit juices and fruit juice drinks

1965
TEDDY BEAR RESTAURANTS, INC.
Cincinnati, Ohio
Drive-in restaurant services

1967
MUTUAL SALES ASSOCIATES, INC.
West Springfield, Massachusetts
Home modernizing sevices

1962
WALTER LANTZ PRODUCTIONS, INC.

Hollywood, California
Chewing gum

1970
GENERAL MILLS, INC.

Minneapolis, Minnesota
Ready-to-eat breakfast cereal

1965
THE REPUBLICAN PARTY OF IOWA
Des Moines, Iowa
Indicates membership

1975
GULF AND WESTERN AMERICAS CORPORATION
New York, New York
Resort hotel services

1974
RELIM PUBLISHING CO., INC.
Chicago, Illinois
Magazines

1967
LYNDEN FARMS, INC.
Seattle, Washington
Poultry products

1970
PLAY-BEAR, LTD.
Skokie, Illinois
Decals

1979
STANLEY H. KAPLAN
New York, New York
Educational services

1978
ANHEUSER-BUSCH, INC.

St. Louis, Missouri
Amusement park rides

1972
ART-ON DESIGNS, INC.

West Bloomfield, Michigan
Transfer paper

1971
DEVONSHEER MELBA CORPORATION

Carlstadt, New Jersey
Melba toast

1967
AUSTIN E. MYERS

Denver, Colorado
Restaurant services

1967
PICTORIAL SPOT-LITE, INC.

Mount Vernon, New York
Luminescent signs and displays

1978
RALSTON PURINA COMPANY

St. Louis, Missouri
Animal feed

1967
BOSTROM CORPORATION

Milwaukee, Wisconsin
Seats for vehicles

1963
GRYPHON CORPORATION

Burbank, California
Motion picture film squeegees

1963
PETIT PIGEON

La Jolla, California
Mail order sales of clothing and accessories

1968
UNIVERSAL CHEMICALS AND COATING, INC.

Elk Grove Village, Illinois
Protective and decorative coatings

1970
TELEDYNE INDUSTRIES, INC.

Los Angeles, California
Engines and motors for land vehicles

1961
DEERE AND COMPANY

Moline, Illinois
Agricultural equipment and parts

PETIT PIGEON

1975
METRO-GOLDWYN-MAYER, INC.

Culver City, California
Education and entertainment

1971
PTARMIGAN INN, INC.

Steamboat Springs, Colorado
Motel services

1976
**ENVIRONMENTAL EQUIPMENT
LEASING COMPANY**

Fort Collins, Colorado
Leasing environmental equipment

1974
**SUBSEA EQUIPMENT ASSOCIATES
LIMITED**

Hamilton, Bermuda
Apparatus and instruments for the development,
exploitation, operation, control, testing, and
maintenance of subsea oil and gas installations

1967
LOUIS RICH FOODS, INC.

West Liberty, Iowa
Refrigerated ready-to-eat turkey

1971
BURTON G. FELDMAN

Chicago, Illinois
Copying services

1973
AGRO LAND AND CATTLE CO., INC.

Tuscon, Arizona
Butchered beef

1968
SWANEE PAPER CORPORATION

New York, New York
Bathroom tissues, facial tissues, paper napkins,
and paper towels

1975
**VOLKSWAGENWERK
AKTIENGESELLSCHAFT**

Wolfsburg, Germany
Automobiles

1976
PENNZOIL COMPANY

Oil City, Pennsylvania
Motor oil, hydraulic fluid, automatic transmission,
lubricant oils and greases, gasoline, kerosene, fluid
oils and solvents

1967
ALTAIR AIRLINES, INC.

Philadelphia, Pennsylvania
Passenger and freight air service

1961
YOUNGS RUBBER CORPORATION

New York, New York
Condoms

1962
CAROLE ACCESSORIES
Los Angeles, California
Real and costume jewelry items

1962
AKRON CATHETER, INC.
Akron, Ohio
Catheters

1979
RALSTON PURINA COMPANY

St. Louis, Missouri
Dog food

1965
EDUCATIONAL DATA SCIENCES, INC.

Fairfield, New Jersey
Providing computerized accounting and record-keeping systems

1974
MOTEL CORPORATION OF AMERICA

Georgetown, Grand Cayman Island
Motel services in connection with operating motel, hotel, inns, and campsites

1977
MOTO-X FOX, INC.

Campbell, California
Lubricants and fuels

1978
TROUSIMIS RESEARCH CORPORATION

Rockville, Maryland
Chemicals for electron microscopy

1976
THE DELEONE CORPORATION

Santa Clara, California
Printed material

1974
THE MENNONITE PUBLISHING HOUSE, INC.

Scottdale, Pennsylvania
Non-technical books of general interest

1974
MERRILL LYNCH & CO., INC.

New York, New York
Financial services

1975
CONTINENTAL CAN COMPANY

New York, New York
Paperboard and corrugated paper boxes

1969
CONSOLIDATED FOODS CORPORATION

Chicago, Illinois
Frozen fish and seafood

1978
CITY OF KANSAS CITY

Kansas City, Missouri
Zoological society

1974
THE W. W. HENRY COMPANY

Huntington Park, California
Adhesives

1960
THE EASTERLING COMPANY

Chicago, Illinois
China tableware

1968
FEDERAL-MOGUL CORPORATION
Southfield, Michigan
Bearings and sleeve-type bearings

World Imports

Import/export distribution channels that opened up during the 1960s gave the average American consumer greater opportunities to purchase imports from around the world than ever before, and brought a romance to products not usually found on domestic soil. Textile and clothing companies, cheese and candy factories, and perfume and cosmetic manufacturers all presented products contrary to the established American style. Much like the products, the foreign trademarks were different, too, reflecting the cultural heritage of the different countries.

Stoic British lions guarded over companies like the Royal Bank of Canada and the Celon Tea Propaganda Board, presenting a sense of safety and stability. Similarly, ornate, flourished typographic treatments expressed the quality and precision of old-world traditions. The trademark of Atelier, the Austrian maker of spectacle frames, adds a clear sense of elegance and craftsmanship to its product; and the Oulevay biscuit man enjoying a bite of himself plays on a sense of humor similar to that we might find in eating an Oulevay biscuit. The subtle stylistic differences found in these foreign trademarks establishes a business and artistic psychology slightly different from their American counterparts.

1968
ALLIED BREWERIES (UK) LIMITED
Burton-on-Trent, England
Ales

1963
OULEVAY S.A.
Morges, Vaud, Switzerland
Biscuits

1968
LABORATOIRE LACHARTRE S.A.

Paris, France
Hair products

1967
B. APRENGEL & CO.

Hanover, Germany
Candy and confectionery

1967
JAKOB SCHLAPFER & CO. AG

St. Gall, Switzerland
Embroidery

1972
PRIMROSE SPORTSWEAR, LTD.

Montreal, Quebec, Canada
Clothes

1960
SOCIETE EMINENCE

Nîmes, France
Briefs, waistcoats, and T-shirts for men, women, and children

1968
CIBA LIMITED

Basel, Switzerland
Chemical preparations for killing weeds

1964
BATHURST CONTAINERS, LTD.

Montreal, Quebec, Canada
Shipping cartons for display purposes

1967
THE DUNLOP COMPANY, LTD.

Birmingham, England
Life rafts

1967
OSHINO ELECTRIC LAMP WORKS, LTD.

Tokyo, Japan
Miniature electric lamps

1969
N.V. NEDERLANDSCHE KABELFABRIEKEN

Delft, The Netherlands
Differential discharge detector

1961
ALLMÄNNA SVENSKA ELEKTRIASKA AKTIEBOLAGET

Vasteras, Sweden
Nuclear reactors

1960
DYNAMIC DISPLAYS, LTD.

Toronto, Ontario, Canada
Assembly systems

1962
THE ROYAL BANK OF CANADA

Montreal, Quebec, Canada
Periodical newsletters

1967
**THE CEYLON TEA
PROPAGANDA BOARD**

Colombo, Ceylon
Tea

1974
FRANZ CARL WEBER-HOLDING AG

Zurich, Switzerland
Toys

1977
JANSSEN PHARMACEUTICA

Beerse, Belgium
Pharmaceutical products for human and
veterinary use

1966
CESKOSLOVENSKE COKOLADOVNY

Modrany, Czechoslovakia
Eating, baking, and cooking chocolate

1967
ATALANTA TRADING CORPORATION

New York, New York
Cheese

1970
**ARTEX S.A. FABRICA DE ARTEFATOS
TEXTELS**

Santa Catarina, Brazil
Beach wear and lounge wear for men and women

1973
**ATELIER BRILLEN ANTON AUGER
GESELLSCHAFT M.B.H.**

Linz, Austria
Spectacles, spectacle frames, and sunglasses

1968
BARTSON'S

Antwerp, Belgium
Clothes

1971
LE CORDON BLEU, S.A.R.L.

Paris, France
Educational services

1974
GAVEAU-ERARD

Paris, France
Upright pianos

1966
**BÄRCHARCITER-VERLAG KARL
VØTTERIE K.G. KASSEL**

Wilhelmsholie, Germany
Phonograph records

1978
GLENMAC KNITWEAR (HAWICK), LTD.

Hawick, Scotland
Knitted cardigans

1973
EXPANSION BIOLOGIQUE FRANCAISE

Paris, France
Cosmetics

1960
ETABLISSEMENTS CHEVALLIER PERE

Angers, Maine-et-Loire, France
Perfumes

1960
L'ALLOBROGE

Chambery, France
Candies

1972
**ÖSTERREICHISCHE HARTKASE
EXPORT**

Innsbruck, Austria
Cheese

1967
CREATIONS PIERRE FERRAT

Paris, France
Clothes

1972
**RUD. STARCKS
KOMMANDITGESELLSCHAFT**

Melle, Germany
Abrasives

1977
RASMUS HANSEN A/S

Copenhagen, Denmark
Cheese

1972
**PULLOVERÅNM SICUEDAD AÑONIMA
INDUSTRIAL Y COMMERCIAL**

Buenos Aires, Argentina
Pullovers, sweaters, sweatshirts, cardigans,
and shawls

1967
J.A. HENCKELS ZWILLINGSWERK AG

Solingen, Germany
Metal household and kitchen utensils

1970
BELLEVILLESURSAONE

Rhône, France
Agricultural machines

1968
INDUSTRI AKTIEBOLAGET

Nasbypark, Sweden
Metalworking machines and tools

1965
IMPERMEABILL SAN GIORGIO SOCIETA PER ASIONI

Genoa, Italy
Clothing

1973
ATELIERS DE LA MOTOBECANE

Pantin, France
Bicycles, tricycles, and motorcycles

1961
RHEINSTAHL HANOMAG AKTIENGESELISCHAFT

Hannover, Germany
Automobiles

1976
MANIFATTURE RIABELLA S.P.A.

Biella, Italy
Yarns and threads

1973
SIMPSON OF AUSTRALIA PTS., LTD.

Victoria, Australia
Men's and women's sports clothing

1967
COMINCO, LTD.

Quebec, Canada
Chemical fertilizers

1977
RUMIANCA S.P.A.

Torino, Italy
Pesticides and plant pharmaceuticals

1969
**J. MAYER & SOHN-CORNELIUS HEYL
LEDERFABRIK AG**

Worms, Germany
Kid leather

1973
AUDI NAU AUTO UNION AG

Ingolstadt, Germany
Automobiles

1960
RADIOTECHNISCHES WERK

Esslingen am Neckar, Germany
Radio transmission

1974
UNICORN PRODUCTS, LTD.

London, England
Sporting goods

1976
PRETAL S.R.L.

Buenos Aires, Argentina
Saddles, girths, headstalls, stirrup leathers, stable
halters, martingales, and reins

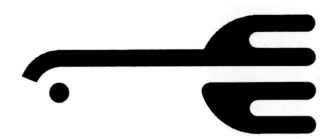

1966
**NIPPON YUSBUTAN KINZOKU
YOSHIOKKI KOYGYO**

Niigata-ken, Japan
Flatware

1960
HEARMANN & REIMER GMBH

Holzminden, Germany
Aromatic and flavoring substances

Sunbursts, Crowns & Globes

The sunburst, crown, or globe implies a universal personality behind a company's trademark without being too specific to its business. These symbols have been incorporated into trademarks since the early twentieth century, and during the 1960s and 1970s they continued to be used by companies that wanted to make claims beyond their local boundaries and establish a broader, worldwide appeal.

An icon throughout history, the sunburst has been used more often than any other mark. Its many symbolic abstractions reference the center of the universe or the soul of the company, and the circular shape suggests permanence, warmth, and comfort.

The crown indicates royalty, the best a company can offer; the product is so exceptional, it is fit for a king or queen. Whether the product is clothing, lumber, or canned fish, the company's mark suggests that the consumer is getting unparalleled quality.

A trademark that represents itself through the image of a globe suggests universal connections. In the 1960s the world, as we knew it, was getting smaller, and corporations were becoming multinational institutions, ever expanding their global presence. A globe somehow suggested that even though a company's headquarters might be in Omaha, their market capabilities were worldwide. Graphic representations of latitude and longitude lines conveyed a more structured, more organized corporate world.

1963
CROWN PAPER BOX CORPORATION
Indianapolis, Indiana
Folding and set-up paper boxes

1965
THE AMERICAN TOBACCO COMPANY
New York, New York
Cigars

1970
THE EMPRESS CORPORATION

Los Angeles, California
Women's and men's sports clothing

1967
EARL SCHEIB, INC.

Beverly Hills, California
Automotive painting and associated services

1960
CLAIROL INCORPORATED

New York, New York
Shampoo

1973
**AZTECA CORN PRODUCTS
CORPORATION**

Chicago, Illinois
Partially prepared Mexican foods

1973
AIFS-DELAWARE

Greenwich, Connecticut
Promoting foreign study

1968
NATIONAL AIRLINES, INC.

Miami, Florida
Air transportation of freight and passengers

1960
IMPERIAL BOOKS

Baltimore, Maryland
Series of books

1964
MASTER MADE PAINTS, INC.

Joplin, Missouri
Paints

1960
CROWN ZELLERBACH CORPORATION

San Francisco, California
Lumber and plywood

1968
**THE MONARCH MARKING
SYSTEM COMPANY**

Miamisburg, Ohio
Blank tags, tickets, and labels sold in roll form

1964
WORLD'S FINEST CHOCOLATE, INC.

Chicago, Illinois
Candy

1968
SPARTANS INDUSTRIES, INC.

New York, New York
Shirts

1963
ROYAL OF PITTSBURGH, INC.

Pittsburgh, Pennsylvania
Jewelry

1968
VINCENT ET VINCENT

Washington, D.C.
Beauty parlor services

1963
PHILIPPINE CIGAR COMPANY

San Francisco, California
Tobacco products

1965
KING FOODS, INC.

Newport, Minnesota
Frozen meats

1972
CHR. BJELLAND & CO.

New York, New York
Canned fish

1969
WINCHELL DONUT HOUSE, INC.

South El Monte, California
Restaurant and snack bar services

1960
C & C PURCHASING CORPORATION

Brookline, Massachusetts
Department store services

1961
CONTROL-PACK, INC.

Anaheim, California
Jams, jellies, catsup, mustard, salad dressings,
meatless sauces, salt, pepper, and sugar

1975
V. R. INTIMATE APPAREL, INC.

New York, New York
Women's clothing

1962
BILT-RITE BABY CARRIAGE CO., INC.

Brooklyn, New York
Doll carriages

1962
THE FULLER BRUSH COMPANY

East Hartford, Connecticut
Hairbrushes and clothes brushes

1961
STOVER PLYWOOD CORPORATION

New York, New York
Refinished plywood panels and plywood doors

1967
THE EARL OF HARDWICKE, LTD.

New York, New York
Drinking and eating ware made of china

1963
THE QUAKER OATS COMPANY

Chicago, Illinois
Biscuits and cookies

1976
SUNHANDLERS, INC.

Cocoa, Florida
Thermal insulating films

1962
MAGIC STAR CHARCOAL

New Lexington, Ohio
Charcoal briquettes

1971
CAMPER CRUISE, INC.

Indianapolis, Indiana
Pontoon boats

1975
SOLAR AUDIO PRODUCTS, INC.

Los Angeles, California
Speakers and speaker systems

1964
**OPTICS INTERNATIONAL
CORPORATION**

Philadelphia, Pennsylvania
Headbands and sun visors

1975
HOWMEDICA, INC.

New York, New York
Pharmaceuticals

1968
THE INN

Bermuda Dunes, California
Hotel/motel services

1971
VIRGIN ISLANDS PUBLIC TELEVISION SYSTEM, CHARLOTTE AMALIE

St. Thomas, Virgin Islands
Educational television broadcasting services

1972
SMITHSONIAN INSTITUTION

Washington, D.C.
Museum services

1966
W. A. BENJAMIN, INC.

New York, New York
Textbooks

1965
SUNSHINE BREWING COMPANY

Reading, Pennsylvania
Beer

1969
FIRST NATIONAL BANK OF BELLEVILLE

Belleville, Illinois
General banking services

1974
RALSTON PURINA COMPANY

St. Louis, Missouri
Recreational services

1970
THE MIDNIGHT SUN, INC.

Atlanta, Georgia
Restaurant services

1961
**PUBLICATIONS DEVELOPMENT
CORPORATION**

New York, New York
Books

1965
COWIES EDUCATIONAL BOOKS, INC.

New York, New York
Reference books

1975
GOLDEN DAWN FOODS, INC.

Sharon, Pennsylvania
Retail supermarket services

1969
MITSUBISHI RAYON CO., LTD.

Tokyo, Japan
Padding and stuffing materials

Keystone

soluna

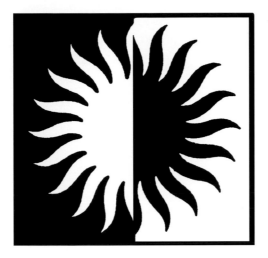

1968
COMFORT GLASS CORPORATION

Miami, Florida
Heat-reflective film products

1967
DAIWA CORPORATION

Gardena, California
Fishing reels and fishing rods

1961
**IMPERIAL HOUSEHOLD
SHIPPING COMPANY**

Long Beach, California
Shipping company

1975
THE SPINNING WHEEL

Blytheville, Arkansas
Bicycle parts

1961
THE PARAMOUNT LINE, INC.

Pawtucket, Rhode Island
Greeting cards

1967
FAIRMONT FOOD COMPANY

Omaha, Nebraska
Carbonated soft drinks and concentrates

1960
**INDUSTRIAL INCOMES, INC.,
OF NORTH AMERICA**

Jackson Heights, New York
Financial services

1968
ACTION PLASTICS COMPANY

Los Angeles, California
Extruded plastic tubing

1969
SID GALPER
Los Angeles, California
Landscape architecture

1966
BENEDIKT MÅSER
Dornbirn, Vorarlberg, Austria
Knitted or woven clothing

1966
MIDLAND INTERNATIONAL CORPORATION
North Kansas City, Missouri
Radio receivers and transceivers, intercommunication sets, batteries, and battery chargers

1970
THE WALTER READE ORGANIZATION, INC.
Oakhurst, New Jersey
Prints and publications

1970
M.T.S. PRODUCTIONS
Cincinnati, Ohio
Automobile bumper stickers and self-adhesive stickers

1966
ASSOCIATED STATE ENTERPRISE
Sofia, Bulgaria
Food and animal by-products

1960
THE GLOBE STEEL ABRASIVE COMPANY

Mansfield, Ohio
Abrasive shot and grit

1963
PERMANENT PEACE ASSOCIATION

New York, New York
Identifies members of association

1962
BLACKWELDER MANUFACTURING COMPANY

Rio Vista, California
Agricultural equipment

1969
INTERNATIONAL BIOPHYSICS CORPORATION

Fullerton, California
Transducers, electrodes, treated pads activated by water, terminals, and parts

1975
PANANGLING, LTD.

Chicago, Illinois
Travel agency services

1967
WHITMAN PUBLISHING COMPANY

Racine, Wisconsin
Magnifying lenses

Your world is
Your reflection of
Your understanding

1974
COMMUNITY CHURCH OF RELIGIOUS SCIENCE
Los Angeles, California
Religious educational books

1968
EDUCATIONAL DEVELOPMENT CORPORATION
Palo Alto, California
Magazine

Entertainment & Leisure

The Dead, the Monkees, Kiss, Heart. By the sixties the evidence of rock 'n' roll's impact on American culture was everywhere. The consumer's appetite for music found sustenance through new technologies like transistor radios, eight-track tape players and color television. As, the baby boomer generation came of age, it discovered new utopias at places like the Fillmore, Woodstock, and Central Park. Our favorite bands of the sixties and seventies were trademarked on albums, T-shirts, posters, and trading cards.

Americans had more leisure time than ever before. Through Saturday morning cartoons, Madison Avenue agencies attracted the attention of our children as consumers and spoke to them with advertisements of model cars, games, comic-book heroes, and action dolls that fed their appetite for entertainment. A quick drive in the car, and you could have a burger from Jack's, Mac, or the King. Whether it was through a friendly figure or well-configured typography, individual groups, as well as companies, were learning of the strength of a well-positioned trademark and its relationship to the consumer's imagination.

1976
PUBLIC BROADCASTING SYSTEM
Washington, D.C.
Broadcasting of educational and cultural television
programing

1965
HASSENFELD BROS., INC.
Pawtucket, Rhode Island
Toy dolls and accessories

CAESARS PALACE

1965
UNITED ARTISTS RECORDS, INC.

New York, New York
Phonograph records

1968
DESERT PALACE, INC.

Las Vegas, Nevada
Hotel and restaurant services

1978
CUSTOM SOUND, INC.

Wichita, Kansas
Retail sound reproduction

1970
BOISE CASCADE CORPORATION

Boise, Idaho
Travel agency services

1973
WARNER COMMUNICATIONS, INC.

New York, New York
Entertainment services

1973
ATARI, INC.

Los Gatos, California
Electronic games

1974
MUSIC MAN, INC.

Anaheim, California
Instrumental speakers and amplifiers

1978
GUITAR INSTITUTE

San Antonio, Texas
Educational services

1966
M. HOHNER, INC.

Hicksville, New York
Harmonicas

1970
ILLAMMEND CORPORATION

Deerfield, Illinois
Electric organs

1966
SCREEN GEMS, INC.

New York, New York
Wallets and small carry-all cases

1960
THE STRAUS BROADCASTING GROUP

New York, New York
Radio communication services

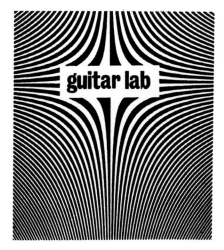

1978
SLASH RECORDS

Falls Church, Virginia
Phonograph records

1973
RSO RECORDS

London, England
Phonograph records and tape recordings

1969
SCHRODER MUSIC COMPANY

Berkeley, California
Phonograph records

1968
CAPITOL RECORDS, INC.

Los Angeles, California
Phonograph records

1964
CHILDREN, INC.

Beverly Hills, California
Phonograph records

1960
THE ELEKTRA CORPORATION

New York, New York
Phonograph records

1971
OVATION, INC.

Glenview, Illinois
Phonograph records

1967
LIBERTY RECORDS, INC.

Los Angeles, California
Phonograph records and albums

1974
VINCE CULLERS ADVERTISING, INC.

Chicago, Illinois
Entertainment services

1978
EMERALD CITY RECORDS, INC.

Norcross, Georgia
Retail record and tape store services

1975
CURT GOWDY BROADCASTING CORPORATION

Lawrence, Massachusetts
Radio broadcasting services

1976
10-4 GOOD BUDDY INNS

Winter Park, Florida
Travel services for citizens band radio users

1978
JOHN KLEMMER

Los Angeles, California
Entertainment services

1977
AVERAGE WHITE BAND

Los Angeles, California
Performance and musical entertainment

1974
MOTOWN RECORD CORPORATION

Detroit, Michigan
Entertainment services

1975
GRATEFUL DEAD PRODUCTIONS

San Rafael, California
T-shirt and entertainment services

1977
HEART

Seattle, Washington
Entertainment services

1977
STARLAND VOCAL BAND

Bethesda, Maryland
Entertainment services

1966
SCREEN GEMS, INC.

New York, New York
Musical entertainment services

1974
ROCK STEADY, INC.

New York, New York
Musical entertainment services

1969
TACO BELL

Torrance, California
Restaurant services

1974
BAR B CUTIE

Nashville, Tennessee
Restaurant services

1960
**TENNESSEE PRODUCTS AND
CHEMICAL CORPORATION**

Nashville, Tennessee
Charcoal briquettes

1961
FOODMAKER COMPANY

San Diego, California
Restaurant services

1972
BURGER KING CORPORATION

Miami, Florida
Restaurant services

1960
JOHN SOUZA

Oakland, California
Salad dressings and sauces

gourmaid

1978
THE DOMAL GROUP
Los Angeles, California
Donuts

1976
AMERICAN SAW & MFG. COMPANY
East Longmeadow, Massachusetts
Hand tools

1972
REYNOLDS METALS COMPANY
Richmond, Virginia
Aluminum foil

1971
AUTOMATIC SERVICE COMPANY
Atlanta, Georgia
Brownies

1974
DUNKIN' DONUTS OF AMERICA
Randolph, Massachusetts
Donuts

1968
MR. DONUT OF AMERICA, INC.
Westwood, Massachusetts
Fillings for donuts

1964
MARK CENTURY CORPORATION

New York, New York
Programming services

1976
SPORT BAIT COMPANY

Olympia, Florida
Fish oil, fishing bait, fishing lures, and fishing
tackle

1969
LAUGH-IN RESTAURANT CORPORATION

Miami, Florida
Restaurant services

1971
CAREFREE TRAVEL, INC.

New York, New York
Travel services to Las Vegas

1967
TOPPS CHEWING GUM, INC.

Brooklyn, New York
Chewing gum

1964
HAWK MODEL COMPANY, INC.

Chicago, Illinois
Toys

ELECTRIC

1969
MATTEL, INC.

Hawthorne, California
Toy miniature automobiles

1971
REVELL, INCORPORATED

Venice, California
Toy model cars in kit form

1968
HERBERT E. BOLTON

El Monte, California
Campers designed to be mounted on pick-up
trucks

1974
R. F. R., INC.

Hope, Rhode Island
Recreational vehicles

1972
MINI-LIMO, INC.

Flushing, New York
Car rental and leasing services

1964
LOUIS MARX & CO., INC.

New York, New York
Toy sports car racing sets

1961
FAIR LANES, INC.

Baltimore, Maryland
Bowling alley services

1972
EURO-BIKE, INC.

Washington, D.C.
Retail motorcycle supply service

1979
HEAD SKI COMPANY, INC.

Timonium, Maryland
Ski clothing and accessories

1975
CONTROL PRODUCTS SURFING EQUIPMENT

Venice, California
Sports equipment and accessories

1979
FIRST AMERICAN WARRANTY CORPORATION

Kansas City, Missouri
Underwriting maintenance and repair insurance
for motorcycle owners

1970
LOVELAND SKIING CORPORATION

Denver, Colorado
Recreational services

1974
MIAMI JAI-ALAI

Miami, Florida
Professional jai-alai competition and betting

1969
HOCKEY CLUB OF PITTSBURGH

Pittsburgh, Pennsylvania
Professional ice hockey games

1975
INFINITY SURFBOARDS

Huntington, California
Surfboards and skateboards

1969
SURF-JET MANUFACTURING, INC.

Lindenhurst, New York
Sport shirts

1970
DORIS MOORE OF CALIFORNIA, INC.

Long Beach, California
Bathing suits, jackets, and shirts

1978
IMAGINEERING, INC.

Tempe, Arizona
Toy novelty items

1976
EN-JAY INTERNATIONAL, LTD.

College Park, Maryland
Beverage recipe cards

1974
THE PURPLE FOOT, INC.

Milwaukee, Wisconsin
Grapes

1978
PARAMOUNT PICTURE CORPORATION

New York, New York
Shirts, footwear, and slacks

1977
TYCO INDUSTRIES, INC.

Moorestown, New Jersey
Train set

Faces & Figures

Faces and figures at times become caricatures of our conditions and relationships in life. The trademarks that represented these companies created an imaginary world where, through these whimsical figures, the consumer could escape the exertions of every day life. Smiling active children, strong construction workers, friendly doctors, and happy, carefree housewives all deliver a similar message: Use our product or service and your life will be free of all troubles. A dialogue is created between the company's figure and the consumer that subconsciously delivers a message to our pop-culture memory banks.

Historical mythic and stoic characters continued to be corporate spokespeople for companies in the 1960s and 1970s as companies brought us more stylized versions of trademarks that were defined with restrained lines and bold shapes. The strength of some of these marks was the graphic designer's elemental interpretation of the positive image and its balance with the negative space around it.

Vanity and fashion products portrayed current styles and attitudes. Hair was an expression of individuality for both men and women. Bow-tied, long-haired, mustachioed men became the trademark for hair creams and apparel, while women with flowers adorning their long, flowing hair and wearing hip-hugging bell-bottoms promoted cosmetics, shampoos, and other personal-care products. The cowboy, Indian, farmhand, Egyptian, pirate, and devil were all incorporated into bold refined symbols that translated the figure into the most current cultural vernacular.

1965

DERMIK PHARMACEUTICAL CO., INC.

Syosset, New York
Mixture of benzoyl peroxide and calcium
phosphate for use in lotions

1962

AMERICAN GREETINGS CORPORATION

Cleveland, Ohio
Greeting cards

1966

**BANKAMERICA SERVICE
CORPORATION**

San Francisco, California
Credit financing services

1968

BANCO CREDITO Y AHORRO PONCENO

Ponce, Puerto Rico
Banking services

1965

**HOMESTEAD VALVE MANUFACTURING
COMPANY**

Coraopolis, Pennsylvania
Installation and maintenance of self-service car
washing equipment

1960

**ARTISTIC CARD PUBLISHING
COMPANY**

Elmira, New York
Greeting cards

1974
THE BAXTER CORPORATION

Paterson, New Jersey
Paper goods and printed matter

1970
HERMON O'LOUGHLIN ENTERPRISES, INC.

Portland, Oregon
Production and promotion of trade shows

1960
STANLEY GREETINGS, INC.

Dayton, Ohio
Greeting cards

1967
NORTH PACIFIC CANNERS & PACKERS, INC.

Portland, Oregon
Frozen french-fried potatoes

1963
T-N-T FOOD PRODUCTS, INC.

Lawrence, Kansas
Unpopped popcorn

1963
DROPPO ASSOCIATES

Springfield, Massachusetts
Advertising agency handling laundromat accounts

1976
THE PIPE FITTER

Madison, Wisconsin
Retail store services

1963
VARIETY HOMES, INC.

Newington, Connecticut
Shell homes and components

The SAVAGE

KATX

Mr. PRINT

Zac-cards

MR. MOD

BURTON
POWER-SNAKE

1971
E & L PRODUCTS
Midway City, California
Seat covers, wheels, brakes, floor mats, and shock absorbers

1960
DECATUR FEDERAL SAVINGS AND LOAN ASSOCIATION
Decatur, Georgia
Savings and loan services

1970
GRAPHICO, INC.
Crystal, Minnesota
Printing services

1960
ZAC-CARDS
Cleveland, Ohio
Greeting cards

1966
MR. MOD SHOP, INC.
New Orleans, Louisiana
Men's cologne

1960
BURTON INDUSTRIES
Tujunga, California
Sewer cleaning

1966
ILLINOIS STATE MEDICAL SOCIETY

Chicago, Illinois
Association services

1964
**LAWRENCE CHILDREN'S UNDERWEAR
COMPANY, INC.**

New York, New York
Children's wear

1960
THE CRACKER JACK CO.

Chicago, Illinois
Marshmallows

1973
DEL MONTE PROPERTIES COMPANY

Pebble Beach, California
Sand

1978
DEW CORPORATION

Tulsa, Oklahoma
Restaurant services

1971
**POCAHONTAS FEDERAL SAVINGS &
LOAN ASSOCIATION**

Pocahontas, Arkansas
Savings and loan association services

1962
WHIRING-PLOVER PAPER COMPANY
Stevens Point, Wisconsin
Fine paper and printers' stock

1964
THE DOW CHEMICAL COMPANY
Midland, Michigan
Dry cleaning products

1965
FABMAGIC, INC.
Santa Ana, California
Rug shampoo

1964
WALKER MANUFACTURING COMPANY
Racine, Wisconsin
Exhaust system parts

1960
NATIONAL CORPORATION SERVICE, INC.
New Orleans, Louisiana
Furnishes uniformed guards, watchmen, and patrol services

1960
BRITISH WEST INDIA AIRWAYS, LTD.
New York, New York
Services comprising transportation, planning, and conducting tours

1960
**FIRST FEDERAL SAVINGS AND LOAN
ASSOCIATION OF KANSAS CITY**

Kansas City, Missouri
Financial services

1960
ST. REGIS PAPER COMPANY

New York, New York
Paperboard cartons

1966
COOL-IT, INC.
Chicago, Illinois
Aftershave lotion

1962
ALLPRINTS PHOTO, INC.
Mansfield, Ohio
Film processing

1974
FINKLER PRIVATE

Grand Rapids, Michigan
Detective agency

1966
SARONG, INC.

Dover, Delaware
Body powder

1967
KAS MANUFACTURING COMPANY, INC.

New York, New York
Electrically operated facial sauna

1968
SEVEN BRIDGES PUBLISHING COMPANY

Chicago, Illinois
Journal of existential psychiatry

1972
COAST BALLET MANUFACTURING COMPANY, INC.

Hollywood, California
Square dance and ballet shoes

1960
COAST BALLET MANUFACTURING COMPANY, INC.

Hollywood, California
Women's shoes

1971
JOE BAILEY AUCTION COMPANY
Dallas, Texas
Auction sales services

1960
EBSCO INDUSTRIES, INC.
Birmingham, Alabama
Floor waxing

1978
BROOKLYN INSTITUTE OF ARTS AND SCIENCES

Brooklyn, New York
Paper goods and printed matter

1960
THE REYNOLDS & REYNOLDS COMPANY

Dayton, Ohio
Accounting services

1962
ROSEBURG LUMBER CO.

Roseburg, Oregon
Plywood

1969
OKLAHOMA CITY TRACTOR COMPANY, INC.

Oklahoma City, Oklahoma
Equipment trailers

1962
PACIFIC METALS COMPANY

San Francisco, California
Welding materials

1968
ASHWORTH BROS., INC.

Fall River, Massachusetts
Card clothing

Let's Talk.

KLEECO

REMARKABLES

Kirsti

IMAGINATION DEVELOPMENT

1971
BEATRICE FOODS COMPANY

Chicago, Illinois
Cookies

1972
CAMELBACK HOSPITAL

Scottsdale, Arizona
Mental health services

1973
KLEECO, INC.

Chicago, Illinois
Drawing paper and boards

1970
MISS MESSENGER, INC.

Wilmington, Delaware
Messenger and delivery service

1969
REVONTULL, INC.

New York, New York
Women's clothes

1967
LORAL CORPORATION

New York, New York
Toys

1969
THE PROCTOR & GAMBLE COMPANY

Cincinnati, Ohio
Shampoo

1970
**MONIQUE'S SCHOOL OF MODELING
AND FINISHING**

South Bend, Indiana
Instruction and training of models

1970
SABASTIAN'S INTERNATIONAL, INC.

Spokane, Washington
Restaurant and tavern services

1978
LORELLE

Seattle, Washington
Costume jewelry sold at home parties

1968
THINK THIN INTERNATIONAL

Long Beach, California
Phonograph records

1968
DE LEON COSMETICS COMPANY, INC.

Omaha, Nebraska
Makeup

1970
MEDIPROD LABORATORIES, INC.

Selma, Alabama
Spray hair cream for men

1972
BESTLINE PRODUCTS, INC.

San Jose, California
Retail sale of home, car, and personal care
products

1970
RIVERSIDE PAPER CORPORATION

Appleton, Wisconsin
Writing papers

1976
LORD REBEL INDUSTRIES

San Francisco, California
Men's clothes

1973
MEREDITH CORPORATION

Des Moines, Iowa
Radio broadcast services

1975
DUNKIN' DONUTS OF AMERICA

Randolph, Massachusetts
Donuts

1975
L.S.K. ENTERPRISES, INC.

Dayton, Ohio
Restaurant services

1968
**RESTAURANTS ASSOCIATES
INDUSTRIES, INC.**

New York, New York
Restaurant services

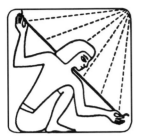

1969
BIOMETRICS, INC.

Cambridge, Massachusetts
Biomedical instrumentation

1978
HERCULES SERVICE CORPORATION

Johnstown, Pennsylvania
Car and truck rustproofing services

1977
THE STRAW HAT RESTAURANT CORPORATION

Dublin, California
Restaurant services

1974
PONTCHARTRAIN STATE BANK

Metairie, Louisiana
Banking services

1976
STIHL, INC.

Virginia Beach, Virginia
Chain saws

1961
BISHOP FREEMAN COMPANY

Evanston, Illinois
Dry cleaning

1966
PENNSALT CHEMICALS CORPORATION

Philadelphia, Pennsylvania
Sodium hydroxide cleaning compound for
cleaning drains

1975
C. ITOH & CO. (AMERICA), INC.

New York, New York
Bicycles

1973
CAYUGA INDUSTRIES, INC.

Ithaca, New York
Construction services

1974
20TH CENTURY CLUB, INC.

Coconut Grove, Florida
Social club services

1966
RED DEVIL, INC.

Union, New Jersey
Hardware and plumbing supplies

1968
PETER MAX

New York, New York
Designer of decorative posters

1976
THE GILLETTE COMPANY

Boston, Massachusetts
Smoke detectors

1900
LIBERTY FABRICS OF NEW YORK, INC.

New York, New York
Lace

1964
THE RATH PACKING COMPANY
Waterloo, Iowa
Refrigerated meats and prepared meat products

1971
PIONEER-STANDARD ELECTRONICS, INC.
Cleveland, Ohio
Electronic components

1972
DYNASTY INDUSTRIES, INC.
Dallas, Texas
Jewelry

1964
THE DETROIT BANK AND TRUST COMPANY
Detroit, Michigan
Commercial and savings banking services

1967
HASTINGS & COMPANY, INC.
Philadelphia, Pennsylvania
Coated plastic films

1970
R. R. DONNELLEY & SONS COMPANY
Chicago, Illinois
Printing services

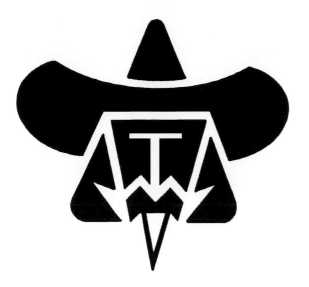

1967
BUFFALO BILL'S STEAK VILLAGE, INC.
Los Angeles, California
Restaurant services

1964
THE AMERICAN TOBACCO COMPANY
New York, New York
Cigarettes

1978
ACE DESIGNING COMPANY
San Francisco, California
Provides temporary technical personnel